VOCAL WARM-UPS

Text by Elaine Schmidt
Tracking, mixing, and mastering by Ric Probst at Remote Planet, Milwaukee
Vocals: Adam Estes & Beth Mulkerron; Piano: J. Mark Baker

To access audio visit:
www.halleonard.com/mylibrary
Enter Code
6670-0901-7357-1234

ISBN 978-1-4234-4583-8

Visit Hal Leonard Online at
www.halleonard.com

Contact Us:
Hal Leonard
7777 West Bluemound Road
Milwaukee, WI 53213
Email: info@halleonard.com

In Europe contact:
Hal Leonard Europe Limited
42 Wigmore Street
Marylebone, London, W1U 2RN
Email: info@halleonardeurope.com

In Australia contact:
Hal Leonard Australia Pty. Ltd.
4 Lentara Court
Cheltenham, Victoria, 3192 Australia
Email: info@halleonard.com.au

Getting Ready to Sing

Singing requires putting the rest of your busy life aside and focusing on both the physical and creative components of making art through sound. Just like athletes, musicians warm up before they practice or perform. Although athletes and singers warm up in very different ways, the purpose of those warm-ups is the same—preventing strain or injury and ensuring that the athlete or musician is limber, relaxed, concentrating, and ready to do his or her best work.

As a singer, you have an advantage over other musicians in that you always have your voice with you, ready to use on a moment's notice. However, that means your musical instrument is in use at all times. Every time you talk, shout, laugh, cry, and even sneeze, your voice is engaged, and not always gently. Everything from pollen, dust, and cigarette smoke to perfume to dry air can take a toll on your voice. Even the simple act of clearing your throat can be rough on your voice.

In addition to using your voice every day of your life, you are also using your breathing apparatus every minute of your life. The same lungs and diaphragm that you rely upon to support your vocal sound are put to hard work when you exercise and are ignored when you slump over a laptop or slouch while watching television.

The following 25 warm-ups are designed to take your voice and body from their everyday habits and routines and to focus and prepare them to sing well. The warm-ups begin with broad, large-muscle relaxation techniques and breathing work that prepare your body. They move on to a gradual, relaxed warm-up of your voice and strengthening of your vocal skills.

Use these warm-ups to ready your mind to sing as well as your body. Keep a pen/pencil and paper handy as you warm up. Whenever a stray, non-musical thought creeps into your head, write it down. You can deal with the things you think of, such as filling the gas tank and returning a phone call, when you're done singing. Writing down those stray thoughts helps you to set them aside and focus on your singing.

Remember, in order to sing well, you must warm up well.

Relaxed Posture

Your posture affects everything you do as a singer, from your ability to breathe well and support sound to the amount of tension you hold in your back, shoulders, and neck. It also affects your audience's perception of you. Careless slouching or frightened rigidity does not convey confidence. You need to stand up straight and give your lungs plenty of room to expand, while keeping your muscles free and relaxed. Step one is to shed whatever tension you brought with you to your warm-up.

To begin, stand comfortably, with your feet about shoulder-width apart and your knees unlocked. Take a deep, relaxed breath. Exhale gently, bending forward at the waist as far as you can without any strain or effort. Let your hands dangle as though you are pointing at your toes, but don't strain or stretch to reach your toes. Close your eyes and let your neck muscles go limp. Think of your body as a soft rag doll.

Notice and enjoy the relaxing sensation of gentle stretching in the muscles of your back and in the backs of your legs. Inhaling slowly, stand back up gradually and smoothly. Think of the incoming breath filling you up, letting that inflation push you back into an upright position one vertebra at a time.

Once you are upright, exhale, sighing gently. Feel free to repeat this process right away and at any time during your warm-up, to ease any tension you may be feeling.

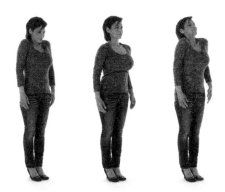

Next, close your eyes, taking a deep relaxed breath and letting out in a long, soft sigh that drops in pitch. Starting at 50, count backward, slowly, to zero, breathing deeply as needed. As you count, relax and roll your shoulders slowly and gently. Then drop your chin toward your chest and let it rest there for a moment. Next, move your head up, as though you're moving your eyes from the foundation to the top of an extremely tall building. Reverse the move, stopping with your chin on your chest.

Without looking up or raising your shoulders, raise your arms above your head and point your fingers at the ceiling. Keeping your arms relaxed, begin shaking them gently. Keep that gentle shaking motion going as you gradually lower your arms to your sides.

Relaxing Your Face

The small muscles of your face need a little attention as well. With your front teeth just far enough apart to insert your fingertip, close your lips and inhale through your nose. Exhale through your mouth, letting your lips part just enough to let out a gentle stream of air while still inflating your cheeks.

Shape your mouth as though you are about to say "oo," as in moon. Exaggerate the "oo" shape as much as you can.

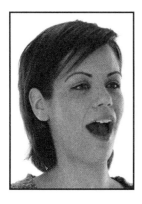

Now take a deep yawning breath, move your mouth slowly from the exaggerated "oo" to a wide-open, dropped-jaw "ah" shape.

Feel the relaxed stretch of your facial muscles. Take a moment and then repeat. You may repeat this exercise at any point in your warm-up or practice session to ease facial tension.

If you decide to use this facial warm-up as a mid-rehearsal or mid-gig relaxation tool, be sure to turn away from your colleagues or hold a sheet of music in front of your face. Aside from creating a rather odd appearance, the yawning face you make could give the unfortunate impression that you are bored to distraction with what's going on around you.

Your last facial exercise is a simple smile. Start by bringing your lips into a smile. Let the smile broaden to spread across your face, until your teeth are showing and you can feel the smile in the skin around your eyes. Let your grin fade to a closed-lipped, subtle smile. That slightly lifted face of your subtle smile will help brighten the sound of your voice.

Breathing

Air and lots of it is essential to singing well. The following exercise will help you relax and expand your breathing apparatus in preparation for singing. It will also get your diaphragm, the muscle that controls your breathing, warmed up and ready to work efficiently. This exercise, performed daily, will gradually expand your lung capacity.

Take a relaxed breath and exhale in a long, gentle sigh. As soon as your lungs are empty from the sigh, inhale through your mouth three times, without exhaling between breaths. Each breath should fill your lungs a bit more. The third breath should make you feel quite full of air. Take two quick sniffs of air through your nose before exhaling in a long, gentle sigh. This warm-up both expands your lungs and rib cage for singing and, thanks to the two little sniffs, raises your soft palate. Repeat the exercise.

You may repeat this exercise for relaxation at any point in your practice session, or in your daily life. Never perform this exercise more than twice in a row, as it is possible to hyperventilate slightly with too many repetitions.

Remember to keep your throat relaxed during breathing exercises and whenever your inhale to sing. A relaxed throat allows you take silent breaths.

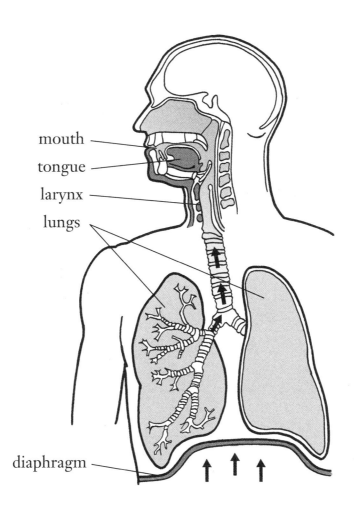

mouth

tongue

larynx

lungs

diaphragm

Engaging the Diaphragm

Nothing wakes up the diaphragm quite like a good, indignant shout of "Ha!" Get a good, deep breath of air and let out a loud, abrupt "Ha!" Go ahead, really let it out. Place your hand on your stomach and feel your diaphragm work as you repeat this quick warm-up a couple of times. Once you are accustomed to the feel of your diaphragm working during this warm-up, you can turn down the volume and use the warm-up without startling anyone.

Stand tall, with one hand on your stomach and the other on your chest. Exhale, then take a high, shallow breath. You should feel your chest rise and your ribcage expand. Exhale again, this time keeping your chest high and your ribcage expanded. Now inhale again, deeply this time. Feel your stomach expand with the breath, too.

Pucker up and blow a strong, fairly short puff of air, as though you are trying to blow out a big candle that's several feet away from you. Feel your diaphragm working both as you inhale and exhale. Do this puff-of-air exercise six times in a row, taking just enough time to breathe between puffs.

Keep your hand in place on your stomach and pant quickly like a puppy for 10–15 seconds. Again, feel your diaphragm working. Don't go any longer than ten seconds at first, as it is very easy to hyperventilate while panting like this.

As long you use a silent "Ha!" sound, you can use the three steps of this warm-up as a way to reinvigorate your diaphragm just before you walk onstage or before beginning a take in a recording session.

Steady Air

In this warm-up and the one that follows, you will focus on creating a steady, smooth air stream that will support your sound as you sing.

Listen closely to yourself as you perform this warm-up. You will be making a soft sound, striving to make it absolutely smooth.

Relax and stand tall. Take a deep breath and let it out in a soft hissing sound. Your lips should be parted and your teeth touching. Listen for lumps and lurches in the hiss and strive to keep the air-stream steady and relaxed to smooth out those uneven sounds.

Take a moment and repeat the exercise using a "th" sound. Take a moment and then repeated the exercise using an "ff" sound.

A silent version of this exercise can be used as a mid-gig breathing tune-up. Moisten your palm and hold your hand, with your palm facing you, about 12 inches from your mouth. Take a deep breath and aim a focused stream of air at the moist spot on your palm. You will able to feel if the air stream is steady or choppy—keep it steady.

Limbering Up Your Sound

The same gentle sigh you used earlier is going to be used for this vocal wake-up. Take a deep, relaxed breath and let out an audible sigh. Although you weren't thinking about singing, you began the sigh on a spoken pitch and essentially slid downward in pitch from there. Breathe and sigh again, this time using that same pitch and singing the sigh. Notice the difference in feel and air support as you sing the downward slide instead of speaking it.

Track 1

Listen to the singer in Track 1 perform this sung-sigh warm-up. Notice that the first and last notes of the sigh are sustained slightly.

Perform the sung-sigh warm-up, choosing whatever starting note feels natural to you. Make the downward slide as smooth as possible and stay as relaxed as you were on the first sigh. Do at least three sighs.

This is also a good relaxation exercise to insert as needed into your practice sessions.

Creating an Even, Supported Sound

The following warm-up is simple and relaxing way to focus your mind and body on creating an even, supported sound.

Tracks 2 & 3

Begin by taking a few deep breaths, relaxing your shoulders and upper body each time you exhale. Listen to the singer on Track 2 as he sings straight tones (notes with no vibrato), striving to make as smooth and steady a sound as possible. The accompaniment is on Track 3.

Mah — mah — mah — mah — mah — mah — mah — mah

This exercise travels well. It can be done without accompaniment anywhere.

For all the warm-ups in this book: If the exercise gets too high or too low for you, if your throat feels tight, if you start straining, or if you can't hit the note, just stop and wait for the exercise to come into your range. After some work, you might be able to go higher or lower. Remember, everyone's range is different. You might be an alto, so the high notes of a soprano are out of your reach, or you might be a tenor and therefore are unable to sing the low notes of a baritone. That's okay. Develop your voice to its unique potential.

The Lip Roll

Singers refer to the following warm-up as a lip roll, lip trill, or lip buzz. It both looks and feels pretty silly. You'll just have to get over that. It's a great way to warm-up all the little muscles of the face that are essential to clear, crisp enunciation. It also helps in developing the smooth, steady stream of air that's essential to producing a good vocal sound and helps you focus and direct your sound.

Listen to the singer in Track 4 she does this exercise.

Track 4

Push your lips forward. Keeping them relaxed and closed, blow a steady stream of air through them and let them buzz. Do this several times until you can sustain the buzz for as long as it takes you finish exhaling. Now hum a pitch and buzz your lips at the same time. No, it's not pretty, but it is effective.

Once you've produced a good, humming buzz, sing the following warm-up along with Track 5, buzzing throughout.

Track 5

Brrr _____   brrr _____   brrr. _____

Singing With a Clear Sound

As you do this and all of the other sung warm-ups in this book, be aware of your posture and breathing. Place your feet about shoulder-width apart, with your knees slightly bent. Remember that standing with your knees locked is not only tough on your knees, it can also cause you to become lightheaded or even to faint. Think of keeping your body weight on the balls of your feet rather than on your heels.

Breathe deeply and silently, relaxing your throat as you inhale and thinking of filling your entire body cavity with air. If it helps to place your hand on your stomach, feel free.

Tracks 6 & 7 Listen as the singer on Track 6 performs this warm-up with several different syllables. As you perform the warm-up with the accompaniment on Track 7, concentrate on making a clear, even, relaxed sound. Alternate the various syllables below, using one for each repetition of the five-note scale.

Mee. _____
May. _____
Mah. _____

In addition to the syllables above, alternate with these as well:

Vee

Nee

Vay

Nay

Vah

Nah

Articulation & Enunciation

This spoken, tongue-twister warm-up is useful before singing and before public speaking. It presents combinations of sounds that are likely to be difficult to enunciate. You will probably discover that some of the tongue twisters are quite difficult for you to say, while others are not challenging at all. Just as some people can whistle and others can't, different people have different speech patterns. Work on the ones that are the hardest for you, to clean up any enunciation difficulties you may have. Pages and pages of other tongue twisters can be found on the Internet.

With each tongue twister, begin slowly and clearly, repeating the phrase several times. You may speed up as long as the phrase remains under your control. If you happen to find yourself chuckling at the results of one or another of the tongue twisters, feel free to have a laugh. Laughing is a great way to engage your diaphragm and shed tension.

How many cookies could a good cook cook, if a good cook could cook cookies?

A Swiss miss on an isthmus at Christmas queries queasy quintuplets.

Three fleeing fleas flew through three freezing trees.

Roll red wagons.

Wicked weather thwarts weary sleuths.

Back black bat.

How many berries could a bare berry bearer carry, if a bare berry bearer carried berries?

Six slimy suckers stuck in sludge.

Reeling real rear wheels.

Whistle thistle sizzle bristle.

Toy boat, boy's boat.

Conquering Consonants

It may surprise you to know that every sound we make when we speak has a name. For the sake of vocal warm-ups, we will deal with a few of the most challenging sounds to sing well.

Continuant consonants, such as m, n, ng, or l can be sustained, or held, as you sing.

Partially voiced consonants such as b, d, g require just brief use of the voice and cannot be sustained as you sing. Fully voiced consonant sounds v, th, z and zh (as in pleasure) require more use of the voice. They can be sustained, but rarely are.

Percussive, consonants don't use the voice at all. The sounds produced for the letters p, t, k, ch can be created without engaging the vocal cords.

The soft sounds made by f, s, sh, and th (in certain cases) are called aspirants, since they begin with a push of air and no vocal sound. Again, be careful not to aim these sounds directly into a microphone, or the rush of air will sound like a windstorm.

> You may want to use the aspirant warm-up to test microphone sensitivity as you are getting ready to work with a new microphone/sound system.

The voiced y sound, when it begins a word, must be sung without an e on the front of it. It may help to think of the exclamation "eeew" as an example of what to avoid.

 Listen to the singer in Track 8 performing the following words on a major scale, placing one word on each note of the scale. Concentrate on making a ringing, clear sound, while enunciating the words clearly as you sing along with Track 9.

Tracks 8 & 9

Man - y   nan - ny   mean - ing   lean - ing   kneel - ing   rail - ing   rain - ing   real.

Continuant Consonants: Many nanny meaning leaning kneeling railing raining real

Unvoiced Consonants: Chair care tar par patty tacky chatty catchy

Partially Voiced Consonants: Bar grill deal Jill good dead jade bread

Fully Voiced Consonants: Very measure zero thy treasure mere Zen then

Aspirant, or Whispered Consonants: Who how flew show three see shy thigh

Diphthongs & Triphthongs

Lyrics matter. Your audience must be able to hear and understand the words you're singing. Just as the production of sound is different for speakers and singers, the diction, enunciation, and pronunciation is also different. To prove this point, say the sentence "I would like to stay at home." Simple enough. Now sing that sentence on one sustained (unbroken) note. It's a completely different ballgame, isn't it?

The first thing you probably noticed when you sang the above sentence was that the words "like" and "stay" are much harder to sing than they are to say. The reason is the two-part vowel, or diphthong, in the middle of the words. When you sing "like," you are singing "lah-eek." When you sing "stay," you are actually singing "stay-ee." The trick to singing diphthongs, as well as triphthongs (three-part vowel sounds) is knowing which of the vowel sounds to sustain.

If you sing the word "like" with an emphasis on the second vowel sound (lah-EEK), you sound a bit like you've just seen a mouse. If you sing it with the emphasis on the first vowel sound (LAH-eek), you sound like a singer who knows what he or she is doing. Likewise, stay should be STAY-ee. Sing them each both ways and you'll hear the difference immediately.

Tracks 10 & 11

Listen to the singer on Track 10, performing the following words to a major scale, placing one word on each note. Sing along with Track 11, making a clear, relaxed sound as you shape diphthongs gracefully. Notice that words that begin with a "w" or "y" sound are also diphthongs. The "w" sound pushes the lips forward into an "oo" position.

Day   say   pray   may   dry   wine   line   cry.

Day say pray may dry wine line cry

Toy boy coin voice out loud down found

Go fro tow slow doe go grow snow

We one went will yes you yet yellow

Tracks 12 & 13

Listen to the singer in Track 12 for a graceful handling of the following triphthongs, then sing them yourself with Track 13.

Flower power   hour tower   fire dryer   wire flyer.

Resonance

The following exercise is designed to take you from the flat, non-resonant sounds of everyday speech to the rich, resonant sounds of singing. For this warm-up, pick a pitch that is comfortable for you, something in the approximate middle of your vocal range. You will use that note for the entire exercise. The exercise is sung at a relaxed, *mezzo piano* (medium soft) dynamic.

Sing the word "ring," holding the "ng" at the end of the word. Note the position of your tongue. Now sing just the "ng" sound, making sure your tongue is touching the backs of your front, bottom teeth. You will feel a little tingle in the roof of your mouth as you sing the "ng".

Keeping the tip of your tongue touching your front, bottom teeth, start by singing the "ng" sound again and move, without stopping, to an "ay" vowel. Take a breath and start on the "ng" sound again, moving to the "ay" and then back and forth between the "ng" and "ay" sounds as many times as you can on one breath. You can feel your vocal resonance open up with each "ay."

Tracks 14 & 15

Listen to the singer in Track 14 as she performs the exercise on a five-note scale, then cue the online audio to Track 15 and try it yourself.

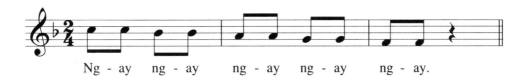

Ng - ay   ng - ay   ng - ay   ng - ay   ng - ay.

Repeat this exercise with any of the following vowel combinations, making sure to use all of them over the course of a week of warm-ups:

- **ng-ah (father)**
- **ng-aa (happy)**
- **ng-eh (then)**
- **ng-ee (bee)**
- **ng-uh (bug)**
- **ng-ih (give)**
- **ng-oh (go)**

Singing Over the Break

You've probably already identified the break in your voice. It is, of course, the distinct line between your chest voice and head voice. The break in your voice is never going to go away. The production of head voice and chest voice is quite different, so there will always be a point at which you have to switch from one to the other in ascending or descending lines. This exercise is designed to help you sing over that break smoothly and easily, minimizing the sound differences between your head voice and chest voice.

Listen as the singers in Track 16 sing over their breaks.

Track 16

Listen to the piano accompaniment on Track 17 and pick a starting point that places your break in about the middle of the scale. Sing along with accompaniment from that point, starting in your chest voice and striving to make the notes on either side of your break sound as much alike as possible. Support is essential and tension is your enemy, so stand tall, plant your feet, keep your knees unlocked, and take a good, relaxed breath before you begin. You may repeat this exercise a couple of times, moving up or down by half steps with the accompaniment, until your break is no longer near the middle of the scale.

Track 17

Mah _____ mah. _____

Flexibility

There is as old adage in theater circles that you should "never let them see you sweat." It also applies to singing. You should never let you audience know that something you're singing is difficult. This means keeping a look of stress or worry off your face and having the vocal flexibility and agility to handle tricky passages.

The next few exercises will work on flexibility, or the ability to move cleanly and accurately through running and leaping passages.

This exercise should be sung quickly and lightly, both articulated and slurred.

Tracks 18 & 19 Listen to the singer in Track 18 perform several options, then choose your own set of syllables, singing along with Track 19.

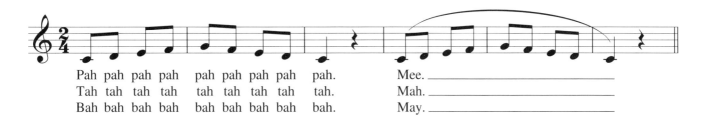

Pah pah pah pah   pah pah pah pah   pah.   Mee. _____
Tah tah tah tah   tah tah tah tah   tah.   Mah. _____
Bah bah bah bah   bah bah bah bah   bah.   May. _____

Singing Accurately

This flexibility exercise works on small intervals, the major and minor seconds. It's very easy to overshoot these intervals, particularly when they occur in fast phrases.

This exercise provides a road map for all of your vocal practice. As a rule, if you can't sing a passage accurately and cleanly at a slow tempo, you certainly can't sing it accurately and cleanly at a fast tempo. Starting out at a slow tempo and speeding up a bit as it becomes more comfortable and secure is a good way to practice any difficult spot in your music. Additionally, placing a syllable on each note of a moving phrase as you're beginning to learn and practice it makes it easier to place the individual pitches accurately. As you get to know the music, you can switch to a legato phrase that is sung on one long syllable.

**Tracks
20 & 21**

Listen as the singer in Track 20 performs this exercise several times slowly then more quickly. Remember to sing this warm-up smoothly, no bumps or unintended accents within the phrase as you sing along with the accompaniment on Track 21. As in previous warm-ups, choose a variety of syllables across the course of a week of practice.

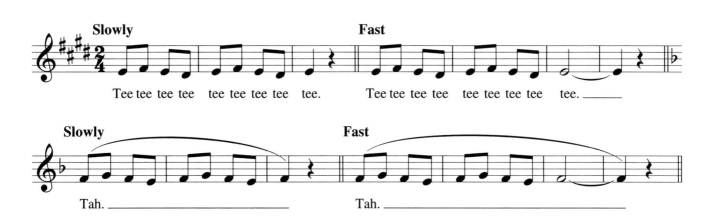

Singing Long Phrases Smoothly

This flexibility exercise works on moving smoothly and cleanly through a longer phrase of moving notes. As in the previous exercise, make sure to sing this exercise slowly and cleanly and then sing it again at the faster tempo, striving for a smooth, clean phrase, free of bumps or accents. Always sing it at least one with individual syllables before moving to the long, sustained, single syllable.

Tracks 22 & 23

Listen to the singer in Track 22 perform both these exercises, first at a slow tempo and then at a faster tempo. Now sing both warm-ups, using the accompaniment on Track 23. Reset the audio track as many times as you need to.

La la la la   la la la la   la la la la   la la la la   la.
La. _____

La la la la   la la la la   la la la la   la la la la   la. _____
La. _____

Phrasing

This exercise warms up flexibility, breath control, and phrasing. Like the previous flexibility exercises, you will sing this slowly and then quickly. When singing it slowly, try to sing the entire phrase on a single breath. If that's not possible for you, take the breath marked in parentheses. Catching a breath in mid-phrase requires that you steal a little time from the note before the breath mark, so that you will be able to place the following note exactly where the music tells you to place it.

Make a nicely arced, graceful phrase at both tempos, with the first note of the second measure as the top of the arc.

Listen to the singer on Track 24 perform this several different ways—taking the marked breath and then without taking the marked breath; using a syllable for every note, and then on an extended "ah" vowel. Experiment with all these options, using the accompaniment on Track 25.

Expanding Your Range

Although your genes are largely what dictate your vocal range, just as they dictate your height and shoe size, you can expand your natural range somewhat through careful, steady work. The following exercise is designed to gently stretch the limits of your range.

Listen to the singer on Track 26 for an example of this exercise.

Track 26

Sing with the accompaniment on Track 27, doing both the ascending and descending versions of this exercise, in a full, supported *mezzo forte* (medium loud) dynamic. The exercise moves up by a half step with each repetition. Listen to the piano accompaniment before you sing and choose a starting point that is comfortable for your voice.

Track 27

As the exercise moves higher, you will begin to feel as though you are reaching slightly for either the highest notes of the little phrase. Once you feel that stretch, sing just one more repetition of the pattern and then stop. Stretching your range is a slow process.

Over the course of a few weeks, you will find that the notes that were too high or too low have become easy to sing. At that point you can go on in the exercise, stretching your range just a bit further.

Singing Legato

Arpeggios are chords that are sung or played one note at a time. The following exercise will give you two arpeggios to sing. Everything should be sung *legato* (smoothly connected), cleanly, with no scooping or sliding.

Listen to the singer on Track 28 for an example of clean, fluid arpeggio singing. The piano-only version is on Track 29.

Tracks 28 & 29

Mah _____ mah. _____

Singing Staccato

This exercise will sound extremely familiar. Now that you have sung the arpeggios in the previous exercise, you are going to sing them again, in a *staccato* (detached) fashion. The important aspects of this exercise are hitting each note precisely, with no scooping or sliding, and releasing the note by stopping the airflow. DO NOT stop the airflow by closing off your throat. Simply stop exhaling and let go of the sound.

Tracks 30 & 31

Listen to the singer on Track 30 for an example of clean staccato singing. Sing along with accompaniment on Track 31. You should stop when the arpeggios reach the edge of your comfortable range.

Ha   ha   ha   ha   ha   ha   ha   ha   ha   ha   ha   ha.

Training Your Ears

These melodic patterns are designed to warm up your ear for harmony. The first phrase consists of the first, fourth, and fifth degrees of the major scale. The chords based on these three scale degrees form the building blocks of countless songs. The second phrase adds a little harmonic color, via the seventh degree of the major scale, and expands the vocal range of the exercise.

Tracks 32 & 33

Listen to Track 32 for an example of clean, fluid singing. Sing along with the accompaniment on Track 33, placing a "mah" syllable on each note, connecting the notes in a *legato* line. Then repeat the exercises on one continuous "mah" syllable. You should stop when the patterns reach the edge of your comfortable range.

Mah   mah   mah   mah.
Mah. _____

Mah   mah   mah   mah   mah. _____
Mah. _____

Once you're mastered these warm-ups in a *legato* style, sing them *staccato* using a "ha" syllable. Feel that diaphragm working!

Dynamics

Tracks
34 & 35

In music, the word "dynamics" refers to how loudly or softly music is played or sung. Changes in dynamics are among the essential tools musicians use for making music meaningful and personal. But employing dynamics takes practice and skill. Listen to the singer on Track 34 performing the American folksong "Hush, Little Baby." Notice the crescendos, diminuendos, and dynamic markings throughout the song. Sing along with the piano in Track 35, using the dynamic markings in the song. Feel free to add more verses, using lyrics you may have learned as a child.

Carolina Folk Lullaby

Hush, lit-tle ba-by, don't say a word, Pa-pa's gon-na buy you a mock-ing bird, and
if that mock-ing bird don't sing, Pa-pa's gon-na buy you a dia-mond ring. And
if that dia-mond ring is brass, Pa-pa's gon-na buy you a look-ing glass, and
if that look-ing glass should crack, Pa-pa's gon-na buy you a jump-ing jack.

Character

Dynamics refer to the volume, the loudness or softness of a note or phrase, but character refers to something a little more refined. A note can be loud and ringing, or loud and harsh. It can be soft and clear or soft and airy. A singer's sound can be aggressive and urgent, or tender and wistful. These alterations in the character of your sound add depth and meaning to the music and lyrics and pull the audience into your performance.

Track 36

Listen to the singer in Track 36 adding distinct colors to the song "Hush, Little Baby."

Take a moment to decide what sort of color or character you would like to give to various lines of the song, remembering that this is an exercise to work on as many vocal colors as possible, not an exercise in giving a performance-ready interpretation of the piece.

Track 37

Sing along with the accompaniment on Track 37, altering not just the dynamics of each phrase, but the color or character of the phrases as well. Give each phrase a different character and dynamic. Have fun with this process and don't be afraid to go overboard in your application of color as you're warming up. The more comfortable you get at adding color to a song interpretation, the more convincing your interpretations will become.

Ready, Set, Relax

Now that you've warmed up the various corners of your vocal technique, it's time for one last relaxing, slurred exercise before you're ready to make some music. Sing several repetitions of this descending exercise, starting slightly above the middle of your range and maintaining a comfortable *mezzo piano* (medium soft) dynamic. Breathe deeply and relax as you sing.

Tracks 38 & 39

This exercise is also a good warm-down that can be used to end your practice session or after a gig. Warming-down relaxes the voice and gives you a moment to collect your thoughts before going back to your daily life. The demo is on Track 38, the piano on Track 39.

Mee.

Practice Songs

The following songs are taken from two very different genres of popular music. "Flow Gently Sweet Afton" is an old Scottish tune favored by folk singers and Celtic groups, while "St. James Infirmary" is an American blues tune that is very popular with jazz musicians. Learn these songs in "straight" version, simply singing the notes on the page. Several fine renditions of both of these songs are available for free listening on the web. Once you know the tunes, listen to how others have performed them and then craft your own interpretations of the songs.

**Tracks
40 & 41**

Flow Gently, Sweet Afton
      Track 40   Demo
      Track 41   Sing-Along

**Tracks
42 & 43**

Saint James Infirmary
      Track 42   Demo
      Track 43   Sing-Along

Flow Gently, Sweet Afton

Lyrics by Robert Burns
Music by Alexander Hume

Saint James Infirmary

Words and Music by Joe Primrose

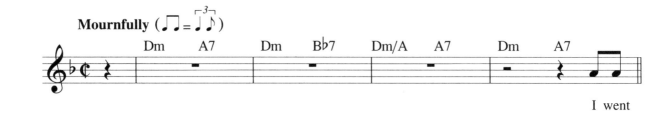

I went

down to the Saint James In - firm - 'ry   to   see   my   ba - by
down to   old   Joe's   bar - room,   on   the   cor - ner   by   the

there.   She was   ly - in' on   a   long   white   ta - ble,   so ___
square.   They were   serv - in'   the   drinks   as   u - sual,   and the

sweet,   so ___   cool, ___   so   fair.   Went   up   to   see   the
u - su - al   crowd ___   was   there.   On   my   left   stood   Joe   Mc -

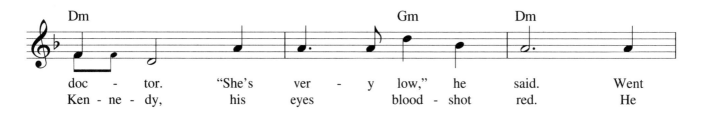

doc - tor.   "She's   ver - y   low,"   he   said.   Went
Ken - ne - dy,   his   eyes   blood - shot   red.   He

back   to   see   my   ba - by.   Great ___   God,   she was   ly - in' there
turned   to the   crowd   a - round   him.   These   are   the ___   words ___ he

Whether you're a karaoke singer or an auditioning professional, the **Pro Vocal®** series is for you! Unlike most karaoke packs, each book in the Pro Vocal series contains the lyrics, melody, and chord symbols for at least eight hit songs. The audio contains demos for listening, and separate backing tracks so you can sing along. Perfect for home rehearsal, parties, auditions, corporate events, and gigs without a backup band.

WOMEN'S EDITIONS

00740247	**1. Broadway Songs**	$14.99
00740277	**4. '80s Gold**	$12.95
00740279	**7. R&B Super Hits**	$12.95
00740344	**11. Disney's Best**	$16.99
00740378	**12. Ella Fitzgerald**	$14.95
00740350	**14. Musicals of Boublil & Schönberg**	$14.95
00740342	**16. Disney Favorites**	$15.99
00740353	**17. Jazz Ballads**	$14.99
00740376	**18. Jazz Vocal Standards**	$19.99
00740354	**21. Jazz Favorites**	$14.99
00740374	**22. Patsy Cline**	$14.95
00740369	**23. Grease**	$14.95
00740367	**25. Mamma Mia**	$15.99
00740363	**29. Torch Songs**	$14.95
00740379	**30. Hairspray**	$15.99
00740388	**33. Billie Holiday**	$14.95
00740392	**36. Wicked**	$17.99
00740426	**51. Great Standards Collection**	$19.99
00740430	**52. Worship Favorites**	$14.99
00740444	**55. Amy Winehouse**	$15.99
00160119	**56. Adele**	$16.99
00109374	**60. Katy Perry**	$14.99
00123120	**62. Top Downloads**	$14.99

MEN'S EDITIONS

00740347	**13. Frank Sinatra Classics**	$14.95
00740453	**15. Queen**	$14.99
00740346	**20. Frank Sinatra Standards**	$14.95
00740358	**22. Great Standards**	$14.99
00740371	**33. Josh Groban**	$14.95
00740387	**40. Neil Diamond**	$14.95
00740399	**43. Ray**	$14.95
00740401	**45. Songs in the Style of Nat "King" Cole**	$14.99
00740439	**56. Michael Bublé – Crazy Love**	$15.99
00148089	**58. Bruno Mars**	$15.99
00740452	**61. Michael Bublé – Call Me Irresponsible**	$14.99
00101777	**62. Michael Bublé – Christmas**	$22.99

EXERCISES

00123770	**Vocal Exercises**	$15.99
00740395	**Vocal Warm-Ups**	$16.99

MIXED EDITIONS

These editions feature songs for both male and female voices.

00740398	**2. Enchanted**	$14.95
00740407	**3. Rent**	$14.95
00740413	**5. South Pacific**	$15.99
00740429	**7. Christmas Carols**	$14.99
00116960	**11. Les Misérables**	$19.99
00126476	**12. Frozen**	$16.99

KIDS EDITIONS

00740451	**1. Songs Children Can Sing!**	$14.99

Visit Hal Leonard online at
www.halleonard.com

Prices, contents, & availability subject to change without notice.
Disney Characters and Artwork TM & © 2018 Disney